THE SEVEN AGES

THE SEVEN AGES

LOUISE GLÜCK

THE ECCO PRESS
An Imprint of HarperCollins*Publishers*

Acknowledgment is made to the editors of the following publications in which some of these poems first appeared: *The American Poetry Review, Gastronomica, The Kenyon Review, The New York Review of Books, The New Yorker, Salmagundi, Slate, The Threepenny Review,* and *Tri-Quarterly.*

HarperCollins books may be purchased for educational, business, or sales promotional use. For information, please write: Special Markets Department, HarperCollins Publishers, Inc., 10 East 53rd Street, New York, NY 10022.

FIRST EDITION

Library of Congress Cataloging-in-Publication Data

Glück, Louise, 1943–
The seven ages / Louise Glück. — 1st ed.
p. cm.
ISBN 0-06-018526-0
I. Title.
PS3557.L8 S4 2001
811'.54—dc21   00-046654

01 02 03 04 05 ❖/QW 10 9 8 7 6 5 4 3 2 1

For Noah and Tereze

CONTENTS

THE SEVEN AGES

Thou earth, thou, Speak.

The Tempest

THE SEVEN AGES

In my first dream the world appeared
the salt, the bitter, the forbidden, the sweet
In my second I descended

I was human, I couldn't just see a thing
beast that I am

I had to touch, to contain it

I hid in the groves,
I worked in the fields until the fields were bare—

time
that will never come again—
the dry wheat bound, caskets
of figs and olives

I even loved a few times in my disgusting human way

and like everyone I called that accomplishment
erotic freedom,
absurd as it seems

The wheat gathered and stored, the last
fruit dried: time

that is hoarded, that is never used,
does it also end?

In my first dream the world appeared
the sweet, the forbidden
but there was no garden, only
raw elements

I was human:
I had to beg to descend

the salt, the bitter, the demanding, the preemptive

And like everyone, I took, I was taken
I dreamed

I was betrayed:

Earth was given to me in a dream
In a dream I possessed it

MOONBEAM

The mist rose with a little sound. Like a thud.
Which was the heart beating. And the sun rose, briefly diluted.
And after what seemed years, it sank again
and twilight washed over the shore and deepened there.
And from out of nowhere lovers came,
people who still had bodies and hearts. Who still had
arms, legs, mouths, although by day they might be
housewives and businessmen.

The same night also produced people like ourselves.
You are like me, whether or not you admit it.
Unsatisfied, meticulous. And your hunger is not for experience
but for understanding, as though it could be had in the abstract.

Then it's daylight again and the world goes back to normal.
The lovers smooth their hair; the moon resumes its hollow existence.
And the beach belongs again to mysterious birds
soon to appear on postage stamps.

But what of our memories, the memories of those who depend on
    images?
Do they count for nothing?

The mist rose, taking back proof of love.
Without which we have only the mirror, you and I.

I call to you across a monstrous river or chasm
to caution you, to prepare you.

Earth will seduce you, slowly, imperceptibly,
subtly, not to say with connivance.

I was not prepared: I stood in my grandmother's kitchen,
holding out my glass. Stewed plums, stewed apricots—

the juice poured off into the glass of ice.
And the water added, patiently, in small increments,

the various cousins discriminating, tasting
with each addition—

aroma of summer fruit, intensity of concentration:
the colored liquid turning gradually lighter, more radiant,

more light passing through it.
Delight, then solace. My grandmother waiting,

to see if more was wanted. Solace, then deep immersion.
I loved nothing more: deep privacy of the sensual life,

the self disappearing into it or inseparable from it,
somehow suspended, floating, its needs

fully exposed, awakened, fully alive—
Deep immersion, and with it

mysterious safety. Far away, the fruit glowing in its glass bowls.
Outside the kitchen, the sun setting.

I was not prepared: sunset, end of summer. Demonstrations
of time as a continuum, as something coming to an end,

not a suspension; the senses wouldn't protect me.
I caution you as I was never cautioned:

you will never let go, you will never be satiated.
You will be damaged and scarred, you will continue to hunger.

Your body will age, you will continue to need.
You will want the earth, then more of the earth —

Sublime, indifferent, it is present, it will not respond.
It is encompassing, it will not minister.

Meaning, it will feed you, it will ravish you,
it will not keep you alive.

We're all dreamers; we don't know who we are.

Some machine made us; machine of the world, the constricting family.
Then back to the world, polished by soft whips.

We dream; we don't remember.

Machine of the family: dark fur, forests of the mother's body.
Machine of the mother: white city inside her.

And before that: earth and water.
Moss between rocks, pieces of leaves and grass.

And before, cells in a great darkness.
And before that, the veiled world.

This is why you were born: to silence me.
Cells of my mother and father, it is your turn
to be pivotal, to be the masterpiece.

I improvised; I never remembered.
Now it's your turn to be driven;
you're the one who demands to know:

Why do I suffer? Why am I ignorant?
Cells in a great darkness. Some machine made us;
it is your turn to address it, to go back asking
what am I for? What am I for?

FABLE

We had, each of us, a set of wishes.
The number changed. And what we wished—
that changed also. Because
we had, all of us, such different dreams.

The wishes were all different, the hopes all different.
And the disasters and catastrophes, always different.

In great waves they left the earth,
even the one that is always wasted.

Waves of despair, waves of hopeless longing and heartache.
Waves of the mysterious wild hungers of youth, the dreams of childhood.
Detailed, urgent; once in a while, selfless.

All different, except of course
the wish to go back. Inevitably
last or first, repeated
over and over—

So the echo lingered. And the wish
held us and tormented us
though we knew in our own bodies
it was never granted.

We knew, and on dark nights, we acknowledged this.
How sweet the night became then,
once the wish released us,
how utterly silent.

SOLSTICE

Each year, on this same date, the summer solstice comes.
Consummate light: we plan for it,
the day we tell ourselves
that time is very long indeed, nearly infinite.
And in our reading and writing, preference is given
to the celebratory, the ecstatic.

There is in these rituals something apart from wonder:
there is also a kind of preening,
as though human genius had participated in these arrangements
and we found the results satisfying.

What follows the light is what precedes it:
the moment of balance, of dark equivalence.

But tonight we sit in the garden in our canvas chairs
so late into the evening—
why should we look either forward or backward?
Why should we be forced to remember:
it is in our blood, this knowledge.
Shortness of the days; darkness, coldness of winter.
It is in our blood and bones; it is in our history.
It takes genius to forget these things.

STARS

I'm awake; I am in the world—
I expect
no further assurance.
No protection, no promise.

Solace of the night sky,
the hardly moving
face of the clock.

I'm alone—all
my riches surround me.
I have a bed, a room.
I have a bed, a vase
of flowers beside it.
And a nightlight, a book.

I'm awake; I am safe.
The darkness like a shield, the dreams
put off, maybe
vanished forever.

And the day—
the unsatisfying morning that says
I am your future,
here is your cargo of sorrow:

Do you reject me? Do you mean
to send me away because I am not
full, in your word,
because you see
the black shape already implicit?

I will never be banished. I am the light,
your personal anguish and humiliation.
Do you dare

send me away as though
you were waiting for something better?

There is no better.
Only (for a short space)
the night sky like
a quarantine that sets you
apart from your task.

Only (softly, fiercely)
the stars shining. Here,
in the room, the bedroom.
Saying *I was brave, I resisted,*
I set myself on fire.

YOUTH

My sister and I at two ends of the sofa,
reading (I suppose) English novels.
The television on; various schoolbooks open,
or places marked with sheets of lined paper.
Euclid, Pythagoras. As though we had looked into
the origin of thought and preferred novels.

Sad sounds of our growing up—
twilight of cellos. No trace
of a flute, a piccolo. And it seemed at the time
almost impossible to conceive of any of it
as evolving or malleable.

Sad sounds. Anecdotes
that were really still lives.
The pages of the novels turning;
the two dogs snoring quietly.

And from the kitchen,
sounds of our mother,
smell of rosemary, of lamb roasting.

A world in process
of shifting, of being made or dissolved,
and yet we didn't live that way;
all of us lived our lives
as the simultaneous ritualized enactment
of a great principle, something
felt but not understood.
And the remarks we made were like lines in a play,
spoken with conviction but not from choice.

A principle, a terrifying familial will
that implied opposition to change, to variation,
a refusal even to ask questions—

Now that world begins
to shift and eddy around us, only now
when it no longer exists.
It has become the present: unending and without form.

Not one animal, but two.
Not one plate, dwarfed by cutlery,
but a pair of plates, a tablecloth.
And in the market, the little cart
neither poignantly empty nor
desperately full. And in the dark theater,
the two hands seeking each other.

Parts of a shrine, like a shrine in church,
blurred by candles.

And whose idea is this? Who is kneeling there
if not the child who doesn't belong,
the blemished one for whom
recess is the ordeal.

Later, bent over his work
while the others are passing notes,
earnestly applying what his teacher calls
his good mind to his assignment—
what is he protecting? Is it his heart again,
completely lost
in the margin at the edge of the notebook?

With what do you fill an empty life?
Amorous figures, the self
in a dream, the self
replicated in another self, the two
stacked together, though the arms and legs
are always perfectly shaded
as in an urn or bas relief.

Inside, ashes of the actual life.
Ashes, disappointment—

And all he asks
is to complete his work, to be
suspended in time like
an orange slice in an ice cube —

Shadows on the dark grass. The wind
suddenly still. And time, which is so impatient,
which wants to go on, lying quietly there, like an animal.
And the lovers lying there in each other's arms,
their shattered hearts mended again, as in life of course
they will never be, the moment
of consummate delight, of union, able to be sustained —
Is it vivid to them? He has seen them.
He has seen, in his singlemindedness, his apparent abstraction,
neither distracted nor frightened away
by all the writhing, the crying out —

And he has understood; he has restored it all,
exalted figure of the poet, figure of the dreamer.

It is discovered, after twenty years, they like each other,
despite enormous differences (one a psychiatrist, one a city official),
differences that could have been, that were, predicted:
differences in tastes, in inclinations, and, now, in wealth
(the one literary, the one entirely practical and yet
deliciously wry; the two wives cordial and mutually curious).
And this discovery is, also, discovery of the self, of new capacities:
they are, in this conversation, like the great sages,
the philosophers they used to read (never together), men
of worldly accomplishment and wisdom, speaking
with all the charm and ebullience and eager openness for which
youth is so unjustly famous. And to these have been added
a broad tolerance and generosity, a movement away from any contempt or
     wariness.
It is a pleasure, now, to speak of the ways in which
their lives have developed, alike in some ways, in others
profoundly different (though each with its core of sorrow, either
implied or disclosed): to speak of the difference now,
to speak of everything that had been, once, part
of a kind of hovering terror, is to lay claim to a subject. Insofar
as theme elevates and shapes a dialogue, this one calls up in them (in its
     grandeur)
kindness and good will of a sort neither had seemed, before,
to possess. Time has been good to them, and now
they can discuss it together from within, so to speak,
which, before, they could not.

When summer ended, my sister was going to school.
No more staying at home with the dogs,
waiting to catch up. No more
playing house with my mother. She was growing up,
she could join the carpool.

No one wanted to stay home. Real life
was the world: you discovered radium,
you danced the swan queen. Nothing

explained my mother. Nothing explained
putting aside radium because you realized finally
it was more interesting to make beds,
to have children like my sister and me.

My sister watched the trees; the leaves
couldn't turn fast enough. She kept asking
was it fall, was it cold enough?

But it was still summer. I lay in bed,
listening to my sister breathe.
I could see her blond hair in the moonlight;
under the white sheet, her little elf's body.
And on the bureau, I could see my new notebook.
It was like my brain: clean, empty. In six months
what was written there would be in my head also.

I watched my sister's face, one side buried in her stuffed bear.
She was being stored in my head, as memory,
like facts in a book.

I didn't want to sleep. I never wanted to sleep
these days. Then I didn't want to wake up. I didn't want
the leaves turning, the nights turning dark early.
I didn't want to love my new clothes, my notebook.

I knew what they were: a bribe, a distraction.
Like the excitement of school: the truth was
time was moving in one direction, like a wave lifting
the whole house, the whole village.

I turned the light on, to wake my sister.
I wanted my parents awake and vigilant; I wanted them
to stop lying. But nobody woke. I sat up
reading my Greek myths in the nightlight.

The nights were cold, the leaves fell.
My sister was tired of school, she missed being home.
But it was too late to go back, too late to stop.
Summer was gone, the nights were dark. The dogs
wore sweaters to go outside.

And then fall was gone, the year was gone.
We were changing, we were growing up. But
it wasn't something you decided to do;
it was something that happened, something
you couldn't control.

Time was passing. Time was carrying us
faster and faster toward the door of the laboratory,
and then beyond the door into the abyss, the darkness.
My mother stirred the soup. The onions,
by a miracle, became part of the potatoes.

Amazingly, I can look back
fifty years. And there, at the end of the gaze,
a human being already entirely recognizable,
the hands clutched in the lap, the eyes
staring into the future with the combined
terror and hopelessness of a soul expecting annihilation.

Entirely familiar, though still, of course, very young.
Staring blindly ahead, the expression of someone staring into utter
    darkness.
And thinking—which meant, I remember, the attempts of the mind
to prevent change.

Familiar, recognizable, but much more deeply alone, more despondent.
She does not, in her view, meet the definition
of child, a person with everything to look forward to.

This is how the others look; this is, therefore, what they are.
Constantly making friends
with the camera, many of them actually
smiling with real conviction—

I remember that age. Riddled with self-doubt, self-loathing,
and at the same time suffused
with contempt for the communal, the ordinary; forever
consigned to solitude, the bleak solace of perception, to a future
completely dominated by the tragic, with no use for the immense will
but to fend it off—

That is the problem of silence:
one cannot test one's ideas.
Because they are not ideas, they are the truth.

All the defenses, the spiritual rigidity, the insistent
unmasking of the ordinary to reveal the tragic,
were actually innocence of the world.

Meaning the partial, the shifting, the mutable—
all that the absolute excludes. I sat in the dark, in the living room.
The birthday was over. I was thinking, naturally, about time.
I remember how, in almost the same instant,
my heart would leap up exultant and collapse
in desolate anguish. The leaping up—the half I didn't count—
that was happiness; that is what the word meant.

ANCIENT TEXT

How deeply fortunate my life, my every prayer
heard by the angels.

I asked for the earth; I received earth, like so much
mud in the face.

I prayed for relief from suffering; I received suffering.
Who can say my prayers were not heard? They were

translated, edited—and if certain
of the important words were left out or misunderstood, a crucial

article deleted, still they were taken in, studied like ancient texts.
Perhaps they *were* ancient texts, re-created

in the vernacular of a particular period.
And as my life was, in a sense, increasingly given over to prayer,

so the task of the angels was, I believe, to master this language
in which they were not as yet entirely fluent or confident.

And if I felt, in my youth, rejected, abandoned,
I came to feel, in the end, that we were, all of us,

intended as teachers, possibly
teachers of the deaf, kind helpers whose virtuous patience

is sustained by an abiding passion.
I understood at last! We were the aides and helpers,

our masterpieces strangely useful, like primers.
How simple life became then; how clear, in the childish errors,

the perpetual labor: night and day, angels were
discussing my meanings. Night and day, I revised my appeals,

making each sentence better and clearer, as though one might
elude forever all misconstruction. How flawless they became —

impeccable, beautiful, continuously misread. If I was, in a sense,
an obsessive staggering through time, in another sense

I was a winged obsessive, my moonlit
feathers were paper. I lived hardly at all among men and women;

I spoke only to angels. How fortunate my days,
how charged and meaningful the nights' continuous silence and opacity.

I had a lover once,
I had a lover twice,
easily three times I loved.
And in between
my heart reconstructed itself perfectly
like a worm.
And my dreams also reconstructed themselves.

After a time, I realized I was living
a completely idiotic life.
Idiotic, wasted—
And sometime later, you and I
began to correspond, inventing
an entirely new form.

Deep intimacy over great distance!
Keats to Fanny Brawne, Dante to Beatrice—

One cannot invent
a new form in
an old character. The letters I sent remained
immaculately ironic, aloof
yet forthright. Meanwhile, I was writing
different letters in my head,
some of which became poems.

So much genuine feeling!
So many fierce declarations
of passionate longing!

I loved once, I loved twice,
and suddenly
the form collapsed: I was
unable to sustain ignorance.

How sad to have lost you, to have lost
any chance of actually knowing you
or remembering you over time
as a real person, as someone I could have grown
deeply attached to, maybe
the brother I never had.

And how sad to think
of dying before finding out
anything. And to realize
how ignorant we all are most of the time,
seeing things
only from the one vantage, like a sniper.

And there were so many things
I never got to tell you about myself,
things which might have swayed you.
And the photo I never sent, taken
the night I looked almost splendid.

I wanted you to fall in love. But the arrow
kept hitting the mirror and coming back.
And the letters kept dividing themselves
with neither half totally true.

And sadly, you never figured out
any of this, though you always wrote back
so promptly, always the same elusive letter.

I loved once, I loved twice,
and even though in our case
things never got off the ground
it was a good thing to have tried.
And I still have the letters, of course.
Sometimes I will take a few years' worth

to reread in the garden,
with a glass of iced tea.

And I feel, sometimes, part of something
very great, wholly profound and sweeping.

I loved once, I loved twice,
easily three times I loved.

The curtains parted. Light
coming in. Moonlight, then sunlight.
Not changing because time was passing
but because the one moment had many aspects.

White lisanthus in a chipped vase.
Sound of the wind. Sound
of lapping water. And hours passing, the white sails
luminous, the boat rocking at anchor.

Motion not yet channeled in time.
The curtains shifting or stirring; the moment
shimmering, a hand moving
backward, then forward. Silence. And then

one word, a name. And then another word:
again, again. And time
salvaged, like a pulse between
stillness and change. Late afternoon. The soon to be lost

becoming memory; the mind closing around it. The room
claimed again, as a possession. Sunlight,
then moonlight. The eyes glazed over with tears.
And then the moon fading, the white sails flexing.

THE DESTINATION

We had only a few days, but they were very long,
the light changed constantly.
A few days, spread out over several years,
over the course of a decade.

And each meeting charged with a sense of exactness,
as though we had traveled, separately,
some great distance; as though there had been,
through all the years of wandering,
a destination, after all.
Not a place, but a body, a voice.

A few days. Intensity
that was never permitted to develop
into tolerance or sluggish affection.

And I believed for many years this was a great marvel;
in my mind, I returned to those days repeatedly,
convinced they were the center of my amorous life.

The days were very long, like the days now.
And the intervals, the separations, exalted,
suffused with a kind of passionate joy that seemed, somehow,
to extend those days, to be inseparable from them.
So that a few hours could take up a lifetime.

A few hours, a world that neither unfolded nor diminished,
that could, at any point, be entered again—

So that long after the end I could return to it without difficulty,
I could live almost completely in imagination.

THE BALCONY

It was a night like this, at the end of summer.

We had rented, I remember, a room with a balcony.
How many days and nights? Five, perhaps—no more.

Even when we weren't touching we were making love.
We stood on our little balcony in the summer night.
And off somewhere, the sounds of human life.

We were the soon to be anointed monarchs,
well disposed to our subjects. Just beneath us,
sounds of a radio playing, an aria we didn't in those years know.

Someone dying of love. Someone from whom time had taken
the only happiness, who was alone now,
impoverished, without beauty.

The rapturous notes of an unendurable grief, of isolation and terror,
the nearly impossible to sustain slow phrases of the ascending figures—
they drifted out over the dark water
like an ecstasy.

Such a small mistake. And many years later,
the only thing left of that night, of the hours in that room.

COPPER BEECH

Why is the earth angry at heaven?
If there's a question, is there an answer?

On Dana Street, a copper beech.
Immense, like the tree of my childhood,
but with a violence I wasn't ready to see then.

I was a child like a pointed finger,
then an explosion of darkness;
my mother could do nothing with me.
Interesting, isn't it,
the language she used.

The copper beech rearing like an animal.

Frustration, rage, the terrible wounded pride
of rebuffed love—I remember

rising from the earth to heaven. I remember
I had two parents,
one harsh, one invisible. Poor
clouded father, who worked
only in gold and silver.

STUDY OF MY SISTER

We respect, here in America,
what is concrete, visible. We ask
What is it for? What does it lead to?

My sister
put her fork down. She felt, she said,
as though she should jump off a cliff.

A crime has been committed
against a human soul

as against the small child
who spends all day entertaining herself
with the colored blocks

so that she looks up
radiant at the end,
presenting herself,
giving herself back to her parents

and they say
What did you build?
and then, because she seems
so blank, so confused,
they repeat the question.

AUGUST

My sister painted her nails fuchsia,
a color named after a fruit.
All the colors were named after foods:
coffee frost, tangerine sherbet.
We sat in the backyard, waiting for our lives to resume
the ascent summer interrupted:
triumphs, victories, for which school
was a kind of practice.

The teachers smiled down at us, pinning on the blue ribbons.
And in our heads, we smiled down at the teachers.

Our lives were stored in our heads.
They hadn't begun; we were both sure
we'd know when they did.
They certainly weren't this.

We sat in the backyard, watching our bodies change:
first bright pink, then tan.
I dribbled baby oil on my legs; my sister
rubbed polish remover on her left hand,
tried another color.

We read, we listened to the portable radio.
Obviously this wasn't life, this sitting around
in colored lawn chairs.

Nothing matched up to the dreams.
My sister kept trying to find a color she liked:
it was summer, they were all frosted.
Fuchsia, orange, mother-of-pearl.
She held her left hand in front of her eyes,
moved it from side to side.

Why was it always like this —
the colors so intense in the glass bottles,

so distinct, and on the hand
almost exactly alike,
a film of weak silver.

My sister shook the bottle. The orange
kept sinking to the bottom; maybe
that was the problem.
She shook it over and over, held it up to the light,
studied the words in the magazine.

The world was a detail, a small thing not yet
exactly right. Or like an afterthought, somehow
still crude or approximate.
What was real was the idea:

My sister added a coat, held her thumb
to the side of the bottle.
We kept thinking we would see
the gap narrow, though in fact it persisted.
The more stubbornly it persisted,
the more fiercely we believed.

Before we started camp, we went to the beach.

Long days, before the sun was dangerous.
My sister lay on her stomach, reading mysteries.
I sat in the sand, watching the water.

You could use the sand to cover
parts of your body that you didn't like.
I covered my feet, to make my legs longer;
the sand climbed over my ankles.

I looked down at my body, away from the water.
I was what the magazines told me to be:
coltish. I was a frozen colt.

My sister didn't bother with these adjustments.
When I told her to cover her feet, she tried a few times,
but she got bored; she didn't have enough willpower
to sustain a deception.

I watched the sea; I listened to the other families.
Babies everywhere: what went on in their heads?
I couldn't imagine myself as a baby;
I couldn't picture myself not thinking.

I couldn't imagine myself as an adult either.
They all had terrible bodies: lax, oily, completely
committed to being male and female.

The days were all the same.
When it rained, we stayed home.
When the sun shone, we went to the beach with my mother.
My sister lay on her stomach, reading her mysteries.
I sat with my legs arranged to resemble
what I saw in my head, what I believed was my true self.

Because it *was* true: when I didn't move I was perfect.

RAIN IN SUMMER

We were supposed to be, all of us,
a circle, a line at every point
equally weighted or tensed, equally
close to the center. I saw it
differently. In my mind, my parents
were the circle; my sister and I
were trapped inside.

Long Island. Terrible
storms off the Atlantic, summer rain
hitting the gray shingles. I watched
the copper beech, the dark leaves turning
a sort of lacquered ebony. It seemed to be
secure, as secure as the house.

It made sense to be housebound.
We were anyway: we couldn't change who we were.
We couldn't change even the smallest facts:
our long hair parted in the center,
secured with two barrettes. We embodied
those ideas of my mother's
not appropriate to adult life.

Ideas of childhood: how to look, how to act.
Ideas of spirit: what gifts to claim, to develop.
Ideas of character: how to be driven, how to prevail,
how to triumph in the true manner of greatness
without seeming to lift a finger.

It was all going on much too long:
childhood, summer. But we were safe;
we lived in a closed form.

Piano lessons. Poems, drawings. Summer rain
hammering at the circle. And the mind
developing within fixed conditions

a few tragic assumptions: we felt safe,
meaning we saw the world as dangerous.
We would prevail or conquer, meaning
we saw homage as love.

My sister and I stared out
into the violence of the summer rain.
It was obvious to us two people couldn't
prevail at the same time. My sister
took my hand, reaching across the flowered cushions.

Neither of us could see, yet,
the cost of any of this.
But she was frightened, she trusted me.

CIVILIZATION

It came to us very late:
perception of beauty, desire for knowledge.
And in the great minds, the two often configured as one.

To perceive, to speak, even on subjects inherently cruel—
to speak boldly even when the facts were, in themselves, painful or dire—
seemed to introduce among us some new action,
having to do with human obsession, human passion.

And yet something, in this action, was being conceded.
And this offended what remained in us of the animal:
it was enslavement speaking, assigning
power to forces outside ourselves.
Therefore the ones who spoke were exiled and silenced,
scorned in the streets.

But the facts persisted. They were among us,
isolated and without pattern; they were among us,
shaping us—

Darkness. Here and there a few fires in doorways,
wind whipping around the corners of buildings—

Where were the silenced, who conceived these images?
In the dim light, finally summoned, resurrected.
As the scorned were praised, who had brought
these truths to our attention, who had felt their presence,
who had perceived them clearly in their blackness and horror
and had arranged them to communicate
some vision of their substance, their magnitude—

In which the facts themselves were suddenly
serene, glorious. They were among us,
not singly, as in chaos, but woven
into relationship or set in order, as though life on earth
could, in this one form, be apprehended deeply
though it could never be mastered.

What joy touches
the solace of ritual? A void

appears in the life.
A shock so deep, so terrible,
its force
levels the perceived world. You were

a beast at the edge of its cave, only
waking and sleeping. Then
the minute shift; the eye

taken by something.
Spring: the unforeseen
flooding the abyss.

And the life
filling again. And finally
a place
found for everything.

THE EMPTY GLASS

I asked for much; I received much.
I asked for much; I received little, I received
next to nothing.

And between? A few umbrellas opened indoors.
A pair of shoes by mistake on the kitchen table.

O wrong, wrong—it was my nature. I was
hard-hearted, remote. I was
selfish, rigid to the point of tyranny.

But I was always that person, even in early childhood.
Small, dark-haired, dreaded by the other children.
I never changed. Inside the glass, the abstract
tide of fortune turned
from high to low overnight.

Was it the sea? Responding, maybe,
to celestial force? To be safe,
I prayed. I tried to be a better person.
Soon it seemed to me that what began as terror
and matured into moral narcissism
might have become in fact
actual human growth. Maybe
this is what my friends meant, taking my hand,
telling me they understood
the abuse, the incredible shit I accepted,
implying (so I once thought) I was a little sick
to give so much for so little.
Whereas they meant I was *good* (clasping my hand intensely)—
a good friend and person, not a creature of pathos.

I was not pathetic! I was writ large,
like a great queen or saint.

Well, it all makes for interesting conjecture.
And it occurs to me that what is crucial is to believe
in effort, to believe some good will come of simply *trying,*
a good completely untainted by the corrupt initiating impulse
to persuade or seduce—

What are we without this?
Whirling in the dark universe,
alone, afraid, unable to influence fate—

What do we have really?
Sad tricks with ladders and shoes,
tricks with salt, impurely motivated recurring
attempts to build character.
What do we have to appease the great forces?

And I think in the end this was the question
that destroyed Agamemnon, there on the beach,
the Greek ships at the ready, the sea
invisible beyond the serene harbor, the future
lethal, unstable: he was a fool, thinking
it could be controlled. He should have said
I have nothing, I am at your mercy.

QUINCE TREE

We had, in the end, only the weather for a subject.
Luckily, we lived in a world with seasons—
we felt, still, access to variety:
darkness, euphoria, various kinds of waiting.

I suppose, in the true sense, our exchanges
couldn't be called conversation, being
dominated by accord, by repetition.

And yet it would be wrong to imagine
we had neither sense of one another nor
deep response to the world, as it would be wrong to believe
our lives were narrow, or empty.

We had great wealth.
We had, in fact, everything we could see
and while it is true we could see
neither great distance nor fine detail,
what we were able to discern we grasped
with a hunger the young can barely conceive,
as though all experience had been channeled into
these few perceptions.

Channeled without memory.
Because the past was lost to us as referent,
lost as image, as narrative. What had it contained?
Was there love? Had there been, once,
sustained labor? Or fame, had there ever been
something like that?

In the end, we didn't need to ask. Because
we felt the past; it was, somehow,
in these things, the front lawn and back lawn,
suffusing them, giving the little quince tree
a weight and meaning almost beyond enduring.

Utterly lost and yet strangely alive, the whole of our human existence—
it would be wrong to think
because we never left the yard
that what we felt there was somehow shrunken or partial.
In its grandeur and splendor, the world
was finally present.

And it was always this we discussed or alluded to
when we were moved to speak.
The weather. The quince tree.
You, in your innocence, what do you know of this world?

THE TRAVELER

At the top of the tree was what I wanted.
Fortunately I had read books:
I knew I was being tested.

I knew nothing would work—
not to climb that high, not to force
the fruit down. One of three results must follow:
the fruit isn't what you imagined,
or it is but fails to satiate.
Or it is damaged in falling
and as a shattered thing torments you forever.

But I refused to be
bested by fruit. I stood under the tree,
waiting for my mind to save me.
I stood, long after the fruit rotted.

And after many years, a traveler passed by me
where I stood, and greeted me warmly,
as one would greet a brother. And I asked why,
why was I so familiar to him,
having never seen him?

And he said, "Because I am like you,
therefore I recognize you. I treated all experience
as a spiritual or intellectual trial
in which to exhibit or prove my superiority
to my predecessors. I chose
to live in hypothesis; longing sustained me.

In fact, what I needed most was longing, which you seem
to have achieved in stasis,
but which I have found in change, in departure."

ARBORETUM

We had the problem of age, the problem of wishing to linger.
Not needing, anymore, even to make a contribution.
Merely wishing to linger: to be, to be here.

And to stare at things, but with no real avidity.
To browse, to purchase nothing.
But there were many of us; we took up time. We crowded out
our own children, and the children of friends. We did great damage,
meaning no harm.

We continued to plan; to fix things as they broke.
To repair, to improve. We traveled, we put in gardens.
And we continued brazenly to plant trees and perennials.

We asked so little of the world. We understood
the offense of advice, of holding forth. We checked ourselves:
we were correct, we were silent.
But we could not cure ourselves of desire, not completely.
Our hands, folded, reeked of it.

How did we do so much damage, merely sitting and watching,
strolling, on fine days, the grounds of the park, the arboretum,
or sitting on benches in front of the public library,
feeding pigeons out of a paper bag?

We were correct, and yet desire pursued us.
Like a great force, a god. And the young
were offended; their hearts
turned cold in reaction. We asked

so little of the world; small things seemed to us
immense wealth. Merely to smell once more the early roses
in the arboretum: we asked
so little, and we claimed nothing. And the young
withered nevertheless.

Or they become like stones in the arboretum: as though
our continued existence, our asking so little for so many years, meant
we asked everything.

After one of those nights, a day:
the mind dutiful, waking, putting on its slippers,
and the spirit restive, muttering
I'd rather, I'd rather—

Where did it come from,
so sudden, so fierce,
an unexpected animal? Who
was the mysterious figure?
You are ridiculously young, I told him.

The day tranquil, beautiful, expecting attention.
The night distracting and barred—
and I cannot return,
not even for information.

Roses in bloom, penstemon, the squirrels
preoccupied for the moment.
And suddenly I don't live here, I live in a mystery.

He had an odd lumbering gaucheness
that became erotic grace.

It is what I thought and not what I thought:
the world is not my world, the human body
makes an impasse, an obstacle.

Clumsy, in jeans, then suddenly
doing the most amazing things
as though they were entirely his idea—

But the afterward at the end of the timeless:
coffee, dark bread, the sustaining rituals
going on now so far away—

the human body a compulsion, a magnet,
the dream itself obstinately
clinging, the spirit
helpless to let it go—

it is still not worth
losing the world.

GRACE

We were taught, in those years,
never to speak of good fortune.
To not speak, to not feel—
it was the smallest step for a child
of any imagination.

And yet an exception was made
for the language of faith;
we were trained in the rudiments of this language
as a precaution.

Not to speak swaggeringly in the world
but to speak in homage, abjectly, privately—

And if one lacked faith?
If one believed, even in childhood, only in chance—

such powerful words they used, our teachers!
Disgrace, punishment: many of us
preferred to remain mute, even in the presence of the divine.

Ours were the voices raised in lament
against the cruel vicissitudes.
Ours were the dark libraries, the treatises
on affliction. In the dark, we recognized one another;
we saw, each in the other's gaze,
experience never manifested in speech.

The miraculous, the sublime, the undeserved;
the relief merely of waking once more in the morning—
only now, with old age nearly beginning,
do we dare to speak of such things, or confess, with gusto,
even to the smallest joys. Their disappearance
approaches, in any case: ours are the lives
this knowledge enters as a gift.

FABLE

The weather grew mild, the snow melted.
The snow melted, and in its place
flowers of early spring:
mertensia, chionodoxa. The earth
turned blue by mistake.

Urgency, there was so much urgency—

to change, to escape the past.

It was cold, it was winter:
I was frightened for my life—

Then it was spring, the earth
turning a surprising blue.

The weather grew mild, the snow melted—
spring overtook it.
And then summer. And time stopped
because we stopped waiting.

And summer lasted. It lasted
because we were happy.

The weather grew mild, like
the past circling back
intending to be gentle, like
a form of the everlasting.

Then the dream ended. The everlasting began.

The windows shut, the sun rising.
Sounds of a few birds;
the garden filmed with a light moisture.
And the insecurity of great hope
suddenly gone.
And the heart still alert.

And a thousand small hopes stirring,
not new but newly acknowledged.
Affection, dinner with friends.
And the structure of certain
adult tasks.

The house clean, silent.
The trash not needing to be taken out.

It is a kingdom, not an act of imagination:
and still very early,
the white buds of the penstemon open.

Is it possible we have finally paid
bitterly enough?
That sacrifice is not to be required,
that anxiety and terror have been judged sufficient?

A squirrel racing along the telephone wire,
a crust of bread in its mouth.

And darkness delayed by the season.
So that it seems
part of a great gift
not to be feared any longer.

The day unfurling, but very gradually, a solitude
not to be feared, the changes
faint, barely perceived—

the penstemon open.
The likelihood
of seeing it through to the end.

RIPE PEACH

1

There was a time
only certainty gave me
any joy. Imagine—
certainty, a dead thing.

2

And then the world,
the experiment.
The obscene mouth
famished with love—
it is like love:
the abrupt, hard
certainty of the end—

3

In the center of the mind,
the hard pit,
the conclusion. As though
the fruit itself
never existed, only
the end, the point
midway between
anticipation and nostalgia—

4

So much fear.
So much terror of the physical world.
The mind frantic
guarding the body from
the passing, the temporary,
the body straining against it—

5

A peach on the kitchen table.
A replica. It is the earth,
the same
disappearing sweetness
surrounding the stone end,
and like the earth
available—

6

An opportunity
for happiness: earth
we cannot possess
only experience—And now
sensation: the mind
silenced by fruit—

7

They are not
reconciled. The body
here, the mind
separate, not
merely a warden:
it has separate joys.
It is the night sky,
the fiercest stars are its
immaculate distinctions—

8

Can it survive? Is there
light that survives the end
in which the mind's enterprise
continues to live: thought
darting about the room,
above the bowl of fruit—

9

Fifty years. The night sky
filled with shooting stars.
Light, music
from far away—I must be
nearly gone. I must be
stone, since the earth
surrounds me—

10

There was
a peach in a wicker basket.
There was a bowl of fruit.
Fifty years. Such a long walk
from the door to the table.

UNPAINTED DOOR

Finally, in middle age,
I was tempted to return to childhood.

The house was the same, but
the door was different.
Not red anymore—unpainted wood.
The trees were the same: the oak, the copper beech.
But the people—all the inhabitants of the past—
were gone: lost, dead, moved away.
The children from across the street
old men and women.

The sun was the same, the lawns
parched brown in summer.
But the present was full of strangers.

And in some way it was all exactly right,
exactly as I remembered: the house, the street,
the prosperous village—

Not to be reclaimed or re-entered
but to legitimize
silence and distance,
distance of place, of time,
bewildering accuracy of imagination and dream—

I remember my childhood as a long wish to be elsewhere.
This is the house; this must be
the childhood I had in mind.

MITOSIS ///

No one actually remembers them
as not divided. Whoever says he does —
that person is lying.

No one remembers. And somehow
everyone knows:

they had to be, in the beginning, equally straightforward,
committed to a direct path.
In the end, only the body continued
implacably moving ahead, as it had to,
to stay alive.

But at some point the mind lingered.
It wanted more time by the sea, more time in the fields
gathering wildflowers. It wanted
more nights sleeping in its own bed; it wanted
its own nightlight, its favorite drink.
And more mornings — it wanted these
possibly most of all. More
of the first light, the penstemon blooming, the alchemilla
still covered with its evening jewels, the night rain
still clinging to it.

And then, more radically, it wanted to go back.
It wished simply to repeat the whole passage,
like the exultant conductor, who feels only that
the violin might have been a little softer, more plangent.

And through all this, the body
continues like the path of an arrow
as it has to, to live.

And if that means to get to the end
(the mind buried like an arrowhead), what choice does it have,
what dream except the dream of the future?

Limitless world! The vistas clear, the clouds risen.
The water azure, the sea plants bending and sighing
among the coral reefs, the sullen mermaids
all suddenly angels, or like angels. And music
rising over the open sea—

Exactly like the dream of the mind.
The same sea, the same shimmering fields.
The plate of fruit, the identical
violin (in the past and the future) but
softer now, finally
sufficiently sad.

EROS

I had drawn my chair to the hotel window, to watch the rain.

I was in a kind of dream or trance—
in love, and yet
I wanted nothing.

It seemed unnecessary to touch you, to see you again.
I wanted only this:
the room, the chair, the sound of the rain falling,
hour after hour, in the warmth of the spring night.

I needed nothing more; I was utterly sated.
My heart had become small; it took very little to fill it.
I watched the rain falling in heavy sheets over the darkened city—

You were not concerned; I could let you
live as you needed to live.

At dawn the rain abated. I did the things
one does in daylight, I acquitted myself,
but I moved like a sleepwalker.

It was enough and it no longer involved you.
A few days in a strange city.
A conversation, the touch of a hand.
And afterward, I took off my wedding ring.

That was what I wanted: to be naked.

THE RUSE

They sat far apart
deliberately, to experience, daily,
the sweetness of seeing each other across
great distance. They understood

instinctively that erotic passion
thrives on distance, either
actual (one is married, one
no longer loves the other) or
spurious, deceptive, a ruse

miming the subordination
of passion to social convention,
but a ruse, so that it demonstrated
not the power of convention but rather

the power of eros to annihilate
objective reality. The world, time, distance —
withering like dry fields before
the fire of the gaze —

Never before. Never with anyone else.
And after the eyes, the hands.
Experienced as glory, as consecration —

Sweet. And after so many years,
completely unimaginable.

Never before. Never with anyone else.
And then the whole thing
repeated exactly with someone else.
Until it was finally obvious

that the only constant
was distance, the servant of need.
Which was used to sustain
whatever fire burned in each of us.

The eyes, the hands—less crucial
than we believed. In the end
distance was sufficient, by itself.

TIME ✓

There was too much, always, then too little.
Childhood: sickness.
By the side of the bed I had a little bell—
at the other end of the bell, my mother.

Sickness, gray rain. The dogs slept through it. They slept on the bed,
at the end of it, and it seemed to me they understood
about childhood: best to remain unconscious.

The rain made gray slats on the windows.
I sat with my book, the little bell beside me.
Without hearing a voice, I apprenticed myself to a voice.
Without seeing any sign of the spirit, I determined
to live in the spirit.

The rain faded in and out.
Month after month, in the space of a day.
Things became dreams; dreams became things.

Then I was well; the bell went back to the cupboard.
The rain ended. The dogs stood at the door,
panting to go outside.

I was well, then I was an adult.
And time went on—it was like the rain,
so much, so much, as though it was a weight that couldn't be moved.

I was a child, half sleeping.
I was sick; I was protected.
And I lived in the world of the spirit,
the world of the gray rain,
the lost, the remembered.

Then suddenly the sun was shining.
And time went on, even when there was almost none left.
And the perceived became the remembered,
the remembered, the perceived.

MEMOIR

I was born cautious, under the sign of Taurus.
I grew up on an island, prosperous,
in the second half of the twentieth century;
the shadow of the Holocaust
hardly touched us.

I had a philosophy of love, a philosophy
of religion, both based on
early experience within a family.

And if when I wrote I used only a few words
it was because time always seemed to me short
as though it could be stripped away
at any moment.

And my story, in any case, wasn't unique
though, like everyone else, I had a story,
a point of view.

A few words were all I needed:
nourish, sustain, attack.

SAINT JOAN

When I was seven, I had a vision:
I believed I would die. I would die
at ten, of polio. I saw my death:
it was a vision, an insight—
it was what Joan had, to save France.

I grieved bitterly. Cheated
of earth, cheated
of a whole childhood, of the great dreams of my heart
which would never be manifest.

No one knew any of this.
And then I lived.

I kept being alive
when I should have been burning:
I was Joan, I was Lazarus.

Monologue
of childhood, of adolescence.
I was Lazarus, the world given to me again.
Nights I lay in my bed, waiting to be found out.
And the voices returned, but the world
refused to withdraw.

I lay awake, listening.
Fifty years ago, in my childhood.
And of course now.
What was it, speaking to me? Terror
of death, terror of gradual loss;
fear of sickness in its bridal whites—

When I was seven, I believed I would die:
only the dates were wrong. I heard
a dark prediction
rising in my own body.

I gave you your chance.
I listened to you, I believed in you.
I will not let you have me again.

AUBADE

There was one summer
that returned many times over
there was one flower unfurling
taking many forms

Crimson of the monarda, pale gold of the late roses

There was one love
There was one love, there were many nights

Smell of the mock orange tree
Corridors of jasmine and lilies
Still the wind blew

There were many winters but I closed my eyes
The cold air white with dissolved wings

There was one garden when the snow melted
Azure and white; I couldn't tell
my solitude from love—

There was one love; he had many voices
There was one dawn; sometimes
we watched it together

I was here
I was here

There was one summer returning over and over
there was one dawn
I grew old watching

The stars were foolish, they were not worth waiting for.
The moon was shrouded, fragmentary.
Twilight like silt covered the hills.
The great drama of human life was nowhere evident—
but for that, you don't go to nature.

The terrible harrowing story of a human life,
the wild triumph of love: they don't belong
to the summer night, panorama of hills and stars.

We sat on our terraces, our screened porches,
as though we expected to gather, even now,
fresh information or sympathy. The stars
glittered a bit above the landscape, the hills
suffused still with a faint retroactive light.
Darkness. Luminous earth. We stared out, starved for knowledge,
and we felt, in its place, a substitute:
indifference that appeared benign.

Solace of the natural world. Panorama
of the eternal. The stars
were foolish, but somehow soothing. The moon
presented itself as a curved line.
And we continued to project onto the glowing hills
qualities we needed: fortitude, the potential
for spiritual advancement.

Immunity to time, to change. Sensation
of perfect safety, the sense of being
protected from what we loved—

And our intense need was absorbed by the night
and returned as sustenance.

SUMMER NIGHT

Orderly, and out of long habit, my heart continues to beat.
I hear it, nights when I wake, over the mild sound of the air conditioner.
As I used to hear it over the beloved's heart, or
variety of hearts, owing to there having been several.
And as it beats, it continues to drum up ridiculous emotion.

So many passionate letters never sent!
So many urgent journeys conceived of on summer nights,
surprise visits to men who were nearly complete strangers.
The tickets never bought, the letters never stamped.
And pride spared. And the life, in a sense, never completely lived.
And the art always in some danger of growing repetitious.

Why not? Why not? Why should my poems not imitate my life?
Whose lesson is not the apotheosis but the pattern, whose meaning
is not in the gesture but in the inertia, the reverie.

Desire, loneliness, wind in the flowering almond—
surely these are the great, the inexhaustible subjects
to which my predecessors apprenticed themselves.
I hear them echo in my own heart, disguised as convention.

Balm of the summer night, balm of the ordinary,
imperial joy and sorrow of human existence,
the dreamed as well as the lived—
what could be dearer than this, given the closeness of death?

FABLE

Then I looked down and saw
the world I was entering, that would be my home.
And I turned to my companion, and I said *Where are we?*
And he replied *Nirvana.*
And I said again *But the light will give us no peace.*